GRACE
ENCOUNTERS

Aaron Erhardt
2019

Dedicated to Sari Eryn Erhardt.

May God bless you to be a woman of faith, kindness, and sincerity. May His grace be abundant in your life and in the lives of those you love.

Contents

Introduction

Victoria Ruvolo was driving home in November 2004 when a 20-pound frozen turkey smashed through her windshield and almost killed her. The impact was so intense that EMTs could not tell if she was a man or a woman. Victoria was rushed to the hospital in critical condition. Nearly every bone in her face was broken, her esophagus was crushed, one eye socket was fractured, and she suffered brain damage. Victoria had to be put in a medically-induced coma, and she spent almost a month in the hospital. Her face had to be completely reconstructed. Victoria's doctors described her survival as a "miracle."

A teenager named Ryan Cushing was responsible for the senseless crime. He was driving around with some of his friends and the frozen turkey, which they had purchased with a stolen credit card, when Victoria's vehicle approached in the opposite direction. Ryan then hurled the turkey at her car. It was a moment that changed both of their lives.

Ryan could have faced 25 years in prison for the offense. He probably deserved more than that. After all, he randomly attacked an innocent woman with no regard for her life. The injuries she suffered were extremely serious. She had to undergo hours of surgery to rebuild her face and endure months of painful rehabilitation. Surprisingly, however, Ryan ended up receiving only six months in jail and five years' probation.

The prosecutor wanted to seek a harsher sentence for Ryan, as did members of Victoria's family. The crime certainly called for far more than six months in jail. Yet that is what the victim wanted. It was Victoria who insisted that Ryan be shown leniency. She had been given a second chance at life and wanted him to get one, too. When Victoria finally met her attacker, she hugged him and said, "I just want you to make your life the best it can be." That's grace.

Ryan should have spent decades in prison to pay for what he had done. That's what his actions demanded. The lighter sentence does not seem fitting or fair. Clearly, Ryan did not receive what he deserved and did not deserve what he received. That's grace.

"Grace" is unmerited favor or undeserved blessing. It is goodwill extended to someone who has done nothing to warrant it. In the New Testament, grace often refers to the favor God bestows on sinners through Jesus Christ. He made a way of salvation possible to us despite our absolute unworthiness. He acted freely and without expectation of receiving anything in return. It was unearned kindness!

Grace can be hard to comprehend in our world of earning. We are used to students earning their grades, scouts earning their badges, players earning their positions, soldiers earning their ranks, and workers earning their paychecks. It is all about getting what is "rightfully yours" based on some form of achievement. That is the opposite of grace. It is not merit-based, but mercy-based.

In the Parable of the Prodigal Son, the older brother struggled to comprehend grace. He felt that since he had put in more time, exerted more energy, done more good, and been more reliable than his younger brother, the party should be for him. He had earned it. His score was higher. His credentials were greater. What the older brother failed to realize, however, is that he didn't deserve his father's goodness, either. He may have worked harder outwardly, but he was harboring animosity, jealousy, and pride inwardly. So rather than resenting his father for extending goodness to someone so undeserving, he should have rejoiced in it.

This is not to say that obedience is unnecessary. Jesus declared, "Not everyone who says to me, 'Lord, Lord,' will enter the kingdom of heaven, but the one who does the will of my Father who is in heaven" (Matthew 7:21). John added, "…whoever does not obey the Son shall not see life, but the wrath of God remains on him" (John 3:36). There are many other passages that make the same point. We must be obedient to please God. However, our obedience constitutes a yearning, not an earning. We are calling out, not cashing in. We should never trust that our own actions merit salvation.

Grace is better experienced than explained. Perhaps that is why the Gospel does not define grace, but rather demonstrates it through the various stories of Jesus Christ. His life was a constant outpouring of divine favor upon an underserving world. The grace He extended to people was practical yet profound. It met them where they were, but never left them as they came.

Grace at a Wedding

There is no mention of how they met, how long they dated, how he popped the question, or who presided over the ceremony. We are not told if it was love at first sight or if it was a friendship that gradually developed into something more. In fact, we don't even know the bride and groom's names. It was an occasion couched in obscurity. Yet this "wedding of unknowns" has become the most-known wedding of all time. Kim and Kanye's might have had star power, but this one had divine power!

The account of this wedding is in John 2:1-11.

> "On the third day there was a wedding at Cana in Galilee, and the mother of Jesus was there. Jesus also was invited to the wedding with his disciples. When the wine ran out, the mother of Jesus said to him, 'They have no wine.' And Jesus said to her, 'Woman, what does this have to do with me? My hour has not yet come.' His mother said to the servants, 'Do whatever he tells you.' Now there were six stone water jars there for the Jewish rites of purification, each holding twenty or thirty gallons. Jesus said to the servants, 'Fill the jars with water.'

And they filled them up to the brim. And he said to them, 'Now draw some out and take it to the master of the feast.' So they took it. When the master of the feast tasted the water now become wine, and did not know where it came from (though the servants who had drawn the water knew), the master of the feast called the bridegroom and said to him, 'Everyone serves the good wine first, and when people have drunk freely, then the poor wine. But you have kept the good wine until now.' This, the first of his signs, Jesus did at Cana in Galilee, and manifested his glory. And his disciples believed in him."

According to *Guinness World Records,* the largest wedding reception of all time took place on September 7, 1995, in India. It was hosted by an actress turned politician for her foster son. There were over 150,000 guests at a cost of more than 23 million US dollars.

My wedding reception was just a little bit smaller than that. Jill and I got married in Gatlinburg, Tennessee, and our reception was at the very classy and elegant Golden Corral. — We had uniformed servants, several different meat selections, and an endless supply of desserts. — It was quite impressive.

The wedding reception in Cana probably took place at a private residence and included most of the community. And it would have lasted much longer than wedding receptions today. They usually went for about a week. William Barclay wrote,

"The wedding festivities lasted far more than one day. The wedding ceremony itself took place late in the evening, after a feast. After the ceremony the young couple were conducted to their new home. By that time it was dark and they were conducted through the village streets by the light of flaming torches and with a canopy over their heads. They were taken by as long a route as possible so that as many people as possible would have the opportunity to wish them well. But a newly married couple did not go away for their honeymoon; they stayed home; and for a week they kept open house" (*The Gospel of John*, Vol. 1, pp. 96-97).

So unlike today, the married couple in that society did not go on a honeymoon. They instead went home and entertained for a week. Among the guests in Cana were Jesus, His disciples, and His mother Mary. In fact, Mary seems to have been more than just a guest. It appears that she was responsible for managing the affairs, since she was notified of the wine shortage and felt free to order the servants around. There is no mention of Joseph.

Though Jesus never married, His presence at the wedding reception shows that He approved of the practice. His attitude was different than that of the Essenes, a prominent first-century sect, who disdained marriage. Jesus knew that God Himself instituted marriage in the beginning for man's benefit, and that what the Psalmist said was true,

"He who finds a wife finds a good thing and obtains favor from the Lord" (Psalm 18:22).

We live in a time when people's perception of marriage is diminishing. Many view marriage like a hot bath — "once you get used to it, it's not so hot." To them, marriage is not a word but a sentence. I saw a joke that said, "Marriage is when a man loses his bachelor's degree and a woman gets her master's degree." Another said, "Marriage is an institution, and who wants to live in an institution?" The truth is, however, when done right marriage is a great blessing. It truly is a gift from God. And wise is the couple who invites Jesus to their wedding!

Jesus was not a social recluse. He was not someone who withdrew from society and kept to Himself. Our Lord was a "people-person" who enjoyed mingling with others. He attended dinner parties at Levi's house (Luke 5), Simon's house (Luke 7), Martha and Mary's house (John 12), and more. As Matthew 11:19 says, "The Son of Man came eating and drinking." Though He was not of the world, He was certainly in the world. It should not surprise us that He would be at a wedding reception.

Marriage Musings

There are a lot of "phobias" out there. Some are more common than others. You have "acrophobia" (the fear of heights), "glossophobia" (the fear of public speaking), and "ophidiophobia" (the fear of snakes). Then you have less common phobias, like "carnophobia" (the fear of meat), "chirophobia" (the fear of hands), "cyclophobia" (the fear of bicycles), "macrophobia" (the fear of long waits), and one I suffered with in school — "bibliophobia" (the fear of books).

Did you know that there is a phobia of marriage? It is called "gamophobia." It is the fear of getting married or being in a relationship. There is also a phobia of not being in a relationship. It is called "anuptaphobia." Here are a few more tidbits about marriage that you might find interesting.

- The first recorded occurrence of a diamond engagement ring was in 1477, when the archduke Maximilian of Austria gave one to his fiancée, Mary of Burgundy. The diamonds were in the shape of her first initial "M."

- Wedding and engagement rings have been worn on the fourth finger of the left hand since ancient times. Do you know why? It was thought that a vein in this particular finger led directly to the heart.

- The white wedding dress started with Queen Victoria in 1840. Before then, brides just wore their best dress. Among the most popular colors in Europe was red.

- The tradition of a wedding cake comes from ancient Rome, where guests broke a loaf of bread over the bride's head for fertility's sake.

- The tradition of a bride carrying a bouquet goes back to the 15th century and was done to mask the smell of body odor in a time when people did not bathe regularly. Most people bathed in May, but they did not get married until June.

- The term "honeymoon" is thought to have come from a Babylonian practice of drinking an endless supply of honey beer for a month after the wedding. It was referred to as "honey month," which led to "honeymoon."

Here are a few "more-modern" facts.

- About 300 couples marry in Las Vegas every day.

- Manhattan is the most expensive place to get married in the United States. The average wedding costs almost $80,000.

- 75% of people who marry partners after an affair eventually divorce.

- A 99-year-old man divorced his 96-year-old wife after 77 years of marriage because he discovered she had an affair in the 1940s.

Wine Shortage

We are not given many details about this particular wedding reception. There was probably a lot of small talk and laughing and horseplay. I don't know what the first century version of the Electric Slide or YMCA was, but you can imagine the guests doing stuff like that. It was a celebration! There may have been speeches and toasts. All we know for sure is that there was wine and, at some point, the wine ran out.

A wine shortage may not sound like a big deal today, but it was a huge issue in that society. The groom's family was responsible for the refreshments, and to run out of wine during the festivities was socially disgraceful. It would bring the family a lot of shame and embarrassment, and they could even be subject to a fine.

Imagine arriving at a wedding reception and being told, "I'm sorry, but we ran out of seats. You'll have to stand." Or, "We would offer you something to drink, but we didn't buy enough cups." That wouldn't reflect very well on the hosts, would it? In fact, the second the car door closed the criticism would probably commence. — "Can you believe that? What an awful party. Who runs out of seats at a reception? Didn't they count how many people were coming?" — A wine shortage in the first century was even worse.

Mary, the Lord's mother, was notified of the problem and immediately turned to Jesus. She came to Him in a panic and said, "They have no wine." I don't think she knew what Jesus would do, but she knew He would do something. He then instructed the servants to fill six large stone jars with water and take some to the master of the feast. By the time he took a drink, the water had become great-tasting wine. He even commented to the bridegroom, "You have kept the best wine until now!"

There is an important lesson for us to learn from the way Mary handled this potential crisis. When the problem arose, she immediately went to the Lord about it. — She did not just wait around hoping things might improve on their own; she did not think the matter was "too trivial" to seek help; and she did not try to rely on her own ability. — She trusted completely in Jesus to handle it.

> "Give all your worries and cares to God, for he cares about you" (1 Peter 5:7, NLT).

Jesus did not have to save the day. It was not His party or His problem. Yet He knew that a family's reputation was at stake. He knew that the newly-weds happy affair was in danger of a cultural catastrophe. Therefore, Jesus did what seemed impossible. He turned large jars of water into wine. That's grace. And it was the best-tasting wine ever! More grace.

Jesus saved a family from embarrassment. He didn't say to Himself, "This serves them right. They should have planned better and not tried to skimp on the refreshments." He just tried to shield them from shame. In that sense, Jesus was a lot like His earthly father Joseph. When Joseph discovered that his fiancée was pregnant by what he assumed was another man, he treated her graciously and tried to ease the embarrassment.

> "And her husband Joseph, being a just man and un-
> willing to put her to shame, resolved to divorce her
> quietly" (Matthew 1:19).

Do we exhibit that same grace toward those in a bind? Do we try to ease their embarrassment or do we add to it? — The person struggling with addiction? The teenager who makes a mistake and turns up pregnant? The foreigner who struggles to speak proper English? The teammate who strikes out and costs you the game? The classmate who is constantly teased because his parents can't afford to buy him nice clothes? The awkward co-worker who struggles to fit in? — Do we ease their embarrassment or do we add to it?

Vertical grace is dependent upon horizontal grace. If we want God to be gracious to us, we must be gracious to one another. James made that very point about a similar quality — mercy. He wrote,

> "There will be no mercy for those who have not
> shown mercy to others. But if you have been mer-
> ciful, God will be merciful when he judges you"
> (James 2:13, NLT).

Two men worked on a large ship. One day, the mate who normally did not drink became intoxicated. The captain seized on the opportunity to harm the mate's reputation by writing in the daily log, "Mate drunk today." The mate was aware of his evil intent and begged him to change the record. The captain replied, "It's a fact and into the log it goes." A few days later, the mate was keeping the log and wrote, "Captain sober today." Realizing the implications of this statement, the captain asked that it be removed. The mate answered, "It's a fact and in the log it stays." — Those who do not give grace will not get grace!

What if you were at that wedding reception in Cana and knew of the wine shortage? How would you have reacted? Would you have made matters worse with your sneering or snickering? Would you have rolled your eyes and walked out? Or, would you have tried to help? If Jesus were not there to save the day, would you have stood up and said, "You know what? I didn't need wine anyway. This is no big deal; we can still have a good time. I'll have some water, please!" — I guess what I'm asking is, "Would you have shown enough grace to overshadow their perceived disgrace? Would that have even crossed your mind?

This miracle is not about a wedding. It is not about wine, either. It is about grace. It is about the Son of God going out of His way to help someone in need. And I am certain that His act of grace had a transformational impact on their lives.

Closing

Jesus did not perform His first miracle in a public setting at Jerusalem, but in a private setting at Cana. Nor did He call for everyone's attention by tapping His fork against a glass or standing up on a chair. There was no fanfare at all. He just quietly met the need of a frightened family. That's grace. He was certainly the "best man" that day!

Grace at a House

Friends are kind of like wing sauce. They come in varying degrees of intensity. For instance, some are "mild sauce" friends. These would be more like acquaintances. You may converse with these people, but you don't really confide in them. They are more of a colleague than a comrade. Some are "medium sauce" friends. These are people you hang out with and do confide in. Your families get together for dinner and you exchange gifts at Christmas, but they are not at the top of your emergency-contact list. They're your buddies, but not your brothers. And some are "hot sauce" friends. These are people who know everything about you — the good, the bad, the ugly — and love you anyway. They have your back no matter what. They're the kind of friends who would drop whatever they are doing to come help you out and not think twice about it. They're your brothers!

Jonathan and David had a friendship like that. They truly loved one another and developed a bond that proved to be unbreakable. In fact, the Bible says that Jonathan loved David "as his own soul" (1 Samuel 18:1, 3) and when Jonathan died, David lamented, "I am distressed for you, my brother Jonathan; very pleasant have you been to me; your love to me was extraordinary, surpassing the love of women" (2 Samuel 1:26). Hence, they were incredibly close.

This is even more remarkable when you consider the fact that Jonathan was the king's son who was supposed to be next in line to the throne, and that David posed an obvious threat to him doing so. It would have been very easy for these two men to be bitter rivals, yet they became best friends. Jonathan put his love for David over himself, his ambitions, and his own family. — They weren't just buddies, they were brothers.

When strife arose between Abram's herdsmen and Lot's herdsmen, the patriarch could have looked out for his own interests and thrown Lot to the curb. After all, he was the "senior statesman" who had received the calling from God, not his younger nephew. However, he defused the situation and humbly deferred to Lot for one reason — "we are brothers" (Genesis 13:8). When Moses saw two Hebrews fighting amongst themselves, he sought to reconcile them for the same reason — "you are brothers" (Acts 7:26). Obviously, Abram and Moses knew what it meant to be brothers. It's about looking out for one another and not letting anything tear you apart.

A good example of friends having that kind of devotion is found in a story recorded in all three synoptic gospels. The lengths these men went to for one of their own show they were more than just buddies, they were brothers. We will look at Mark's account.

> "And when he returned to Capernaum after some
> days, it was reported that he was at home. And many
> were gathered together, so that there was no more
> room, not even at the door. And he was preaching

the word to them. And they came, bringing to him a paralytic carried by four men. And when they could not get near him because of the crowd, they removed the roof above him, and when they had made an opening, they let down the bed on which the paralytic lay. And when Jesus saw their faith, he said to the paralytic, 'Son, your sins are forgiven.' Now some of the scribes were sitting there, questioning in their hearts, 'Why does this man speak like that? He is blaspheming! Who can forgive sins but God alone?' And immediately Jesus, perceiving in his spirit that they thus questioned within themselves, said to them, 'Why do you question these things in your hearts? Which is easier, to say to the paralytic, 'Your sins are forgiven,' or to say, 'Rise, take up your bed and walk'? But that you may know that the Son of Man has authority on earth to forgive sins' — he said to the paralytic — 'I say to you, rise, pick up your bed, and go home.' And he rose and immediately picked up his bed and went out before them all, so that they were all amazed and glorified God, saying, 'We never saw anything like this'" (Mark 2:1-12)!

"Capernaum" was a village located on the northwest edge of the Sea of Galilee. It was a prosperous fishing community where Peter, Andrew, James, and John ran their business. It was also where Matthew worked as a tax collector. Capernaum became Jesus' headquarters during His Galilean ministry, even though He later rebuked the people there for being worse than Sodom (Matthew 11:23).

When Jesus returned to Capernaum, large crowds began to gather at the house where He was staying (probably Peter's house). It was so packed that they were "jamming the entrance so no one could get in or out" (MSG). Jesus used this opportunity to teach, and as He was doing so four men arrived carrying a stretcher.

We are not told the four men's names, ages, or how far they had travelled. Was it a few houses? A few blocks? A few miles? All we know is that they were carrying their friend who was paralyzed. He was bedridden and had to completely rely on others. This was not only a terrible condition, but in that society disease and disability were generally assumed to be the direct consequence of sin. So, there was a stigma he had to deal with as well. Though people were probably sympathetic, they would have been suspicious as they wondered within themselves what awful deed he (or someone close to him) had done.

The four men tried to push and nudge their way through the front door, but they soon realized that it was hopeless. The place was just too crowded to get inside. Therefore, they had a choice to make — give up or press on? For these men, giving up was simply not an option.

At first light on September 13, 1814, British warships began firing a barrage of bombs and rockets at Fort McHenry in Baltimore. This was perhaps the most pivotal moment in the on-going war of 1812. Just weeks earlier, the British had successfully attacked Washington D.C., burning down the Capitol, the Treasury Building, and the Presidential Mansion. If Fort McHenry fell, the city of Baltimore would be easy prey and the American's morale would be crushed.

The warship's bombardment of Fort McHenry was an early nineteenth-century version of "shock and awe." More than 1,500 rounds were fired at the fort for 25 straight hours. A local newspaper article described the scene in Baltimore like this: "The houses in the city were shaken to their foundations, for never, perhaps from the time of invention of cannon to the present day, were number of pieces fired with so rapid succession."

In addition to the relentless bombing, weather conditions worsened throughout the day and heavy storms pounded the area. As night set in, an order was given to extinguish all lights in Baltimore to prevent the British from hitting their targets. All you could see was the periodic flashes of lightning and bombs bursting in air. A British midshipman stated, "All the night the bombardment continued with unabated vigor. The hissing of rockets and the fiery shells glittered in the air, threatening destruction as they fell."

Remarkably, as night gave way to dawn's early light the stars and stripes were still waving above the fort. Though severely outgunned, the Americans had refused to lower their flag. They held their ground and did not surrender. That's determination.

Though the challenge before them was obviously not as daunting as what the Americans faced at Fort McHenry, the four men who brought their friend to see Jesus exhibited a similar degree of determination. They too were unwilling to give up or stand down. Surrender was simply not an option!

The men noticed an outside stairway leading up to the roof and decided to take some drastic measures. They would carry their friend up the narrow stairway, dig through the roof with their own hands, and lower him down to Jesus.

Houses in Palestine were usually built with flat roofs made of mortar, sand, ash, and tar bound together and covered with tiles. However, just getting their friend up the stairs would be a challenge. After all, they were probably exhausted from carrying a grown man through the streets, and now they would have to hold the stretcher up and keep it level as they climbed a narrow staircase to the roof. What if one of them tripped going up the stairs, or what if they didn't keep the stretcher level? Their friend would have fallen.

Once they made it up the stairs, the men got down on their knees and began removing the roof. They pulled up the tiles and dug through the underlying layer of material. I wonder what it was like for Jesus and the others in the house below. They probably heard the footsteps and clawing sounds, and then saw pieces of debris start to fall as a small hole emerged. And before long, there was an opening so large that it was big enough to lower a stretcher through.

The men had trespassed by going up on the roof without permission and damaged someone else's personal property by tearing a big hole in it. Why would they do that? Because the men knew that if they could carry their friend to Jesus but one time, they would never have to carry him again. Buddies might not be willing to go that far, but brothers do! The men then took their sashes, tied them to the four ends of the stretcher, and lowered the paralytic inside the house.

What if one of the sashes was not tied tightly enough and it came loose? What if one of the men let his end down faster than the others? What if Jesus was not happy with the men for destroying property and interrupting a Bible study? This was a risky plan. There was a lot that could have gone wrong. These men were clearly "going for broke" at this point.

When the paralytic made it down to the Lord, everyone waited anxiously to see how He would respond. All eyes, including the four sets gazing from the roof, were fixed on Him. Would He be receptive to the men or rebuke them for not coming earlier or waiting until later? If anyone had those concerns, they were quickly proven to be unfounded. Jesus was not upset; He was impressed. He was pleased with the degree of faith these men had shown and responded favorably. That's grace.

Jesus first dealt with the paralytic's most important need — his spiritual condition. He boldly declared that the man's sins were forgiven. Then He said, "Rise, pick up your bed, and go home."

Amazingly, the man who had never walked before suddenly sat up, stood up, and snatched up his stretcher. He was healed instantly and completely. Without any rehab or therapy, he had the ability to walk normally. His bones, joints, muscles, nerves, and tendons were fully restored, and he had full control of his coordination and balance. There was no stumbling or fumbling, he had been made well by the Great Physician. That's grace.

Closing

The paralytic went from weak to strong, from broken to fixed, and from guilty to innocent. He left much differently than he had come. That's what an encounter with Jesus usually did. He was set free from the chains that had bound him for so long, both physically and spiritually. And the only hero more impressive than his four friends was the Physician they brought him to see!

Grace at a Funeral

A 6-year-old boy named Ayden Roberts was killed in a violent crash involving three cars in southern Indiana. His father ran off the road, overcorrected, and then collided with oncoming traffic. It was another traumatic loss for a family that was already suffering terribly. Just two months earlier, Ayden's younger brother had drowned in a nearby creek. A double tragedy.

In May of 2017, a minister in central Kentucky lost both of his parents and a child in an accident on the Bluegrass Parkway in Nelson County. They were on their way to see a flower garden when a semi crossed the median and struck their vehicle. A double tragedy.

Jesus once encountered a woman who had suffered a double tragedy. First, she lost her husband. He was the love of her life; the man she adored and hoped to grow old with. He was her best friend, financial provider, and the father of their child. Yet he had been taken tragically. Then she lost her son. Her only son. He was the center of her universe and the one part of her husband that lived on. The child was not only going to be her means of support in the years to come, he was her sole hope of perpetuating the family line. However, he too was gone. Can you even imagine? — This woman was in trouble!

When Jesus met this woman, she was part of her son's funeral procession. As they were going out of the town gate, Jesus and His disciples were coming in the town gate. The story is found in Luke 7:11-17.

> "Soon afterward he went to a town called Nain, and his disciples and a great crowd went with him. As he drew near to the gate of the town, behold, a man who had died was being carried out, the only son of his mother, and she was a widow, and a considerable crowd from the town was with her. And when the Lord saw her, he had compassion on her and said to her, 'Do not weep.' Then he came up and touched the bier, and the bearers stood still. And he said, 'Young man, I say to you, arise.' And the dead man sat up and began to speak, and Jesus gave him to his mother. Fear seized them all, and they glorified God, saying, 'A great prophet has arisen among us!' and 'God has visited his people!' And this report about him spread through the whole of Judea and all the surrounding country."

"Nain" was a small village in Galilee. It was about 6 miles southeast of Nazareth and 20 miles from Capernaum. It was there that Jesus had healed the Centurion's servant just hours earlier. As Jesus entered Nain with a large crowd surrounding Him, He ran into another large crowd. Their demeanors, however, could not have been more different. The people with Jesus were full of joy and excitement. They were still buzzing from the miracle He had just performed. The people in the other crowd were full of sadness and despair. They were part of a funeral procession.

The funeral procession would have consisted of relatives, close friends, and professional mourners. (Even the poorest Jews were expected to hire at least two musicians and one wailing woman). The mourners would shriek and pound their breasts as the corpse was carried on a wooden slab to a burial place outside of town.

We do not know the deceased person's name or age, though Jesus does refer to him as a "young" man. That term in Greek describes a youth in the prime of life, under the age of 40. Nor do we know how he died. We are not told if it was a prolonged illness or a sudden accident. All we know is that he was an only child.

There is a unique bond that exists between parents and children. Parents will do things for their kids that they would not do for anyone else. For instance, a good mom and dad will sit for hours in a hot auditorium to watch their kid play what amounts to a stage prop in the school production, and then brag about it all week. Parents will smile and wave at their child dozens of times as he passes by on the merry-go-round, travel from store to store in search of the perfect outfit, and pay thousands of dollars in college tuition. — The umbilical chord may be detached, but the bond always remains. You can only imagine then how this woman must have felt.

Though the woman was surrounded by lots of people at that moment, within a short period of time they would all be gone. They would all go back to living their lives. They would all return to their families and jobs and regular routines. But not her. She would go home to an empty house, where the silence would be deafening and the memories unbearable. While their lives would get back to normal, her life would never be the same.

Steve Sebree, an elder of the church in Louisville, lost his only son a few years ago. It has obviously been the most difficult part of his life, and you don't have to be around him and his wife long to sense their loss. Steve posted this reminder on his *Facebook* page one Mother's Day:

> "Some moms are struggling today, thinking this day no longer belongs to them, but it does. Once a mom, always a mom. Honor and commend them for their love and devotion for the child they lost and let them know they deserve to celebrate, too. Grey HAS the best mom ever!"

In addition to the emotional pain this woman faced, there were economic concerns. In that society, there was no government assistance or any charitable organizations to provide for her needs. A woman without a husband or son to support her would probably be reduced to begging on the streets. As I said, this woman was in trouble.

The Jews usually buried people within 24 hours. They did not practice embalming, so everything was done in haste. This means the young man had literally just passed away. The mother was probably still in a degree of shock, not having had the time to digest everything. It all must have seemed so surreal. And then she saw Jesus.

Jesus did not just pass by the procession or stand off to the side in respectful silence. He felt the mother's pain. His heart broke for hers. He walked up to the woman and said, "Do not weep." That was His way of saying, "It will be okay." Here we are reminded that we serve a sensitive Savior, a compassionate Christ, who really does sympathize with our struggles.

When God spoke to Hezekiah in 2 Kings 20:5, He said, "I have heard your prayer; I have seen your tears." Isn't that a comforting thought? The Sovereign and Majestic Monarch of the Universe was not too big or too busy to notice Hezekiah's crying. God saw his tears! And Jesus saw this woman's tears.

Compassion was an intricate part of the Lord's teachings. In the parable of the Unforgiving Servant, the master had compassion on his subordinate and forgave the man's debt (Matthew 18:27); the Good Samaritan had compassion on the injured traveler (Luke 10:33); and the prodigal son's father had compassion on him (Luke 15:20). Compassion was also part of the beatitudes (Matthew 5:7) and is stressed throughout the New Testament (Ephesians 4:32; Colossians 3:12; 1 Peter 3:8). Interestingly, however, compassion was not exactly a prevalent practice in the "dog eat dog" society in which Jesus lived. Though we are not surprised by the Lord's compassion, the woman probably was!

President William McKinley had a difficult time choosing between two candidates for ambassador. Their qualifications were almost equal and he sought something that would set one of them apart. He recalled an incident years earlier on a street car at rush hour. A woman carrying a heavy basket boarded the car but could not find a seat. She was forced to stand as the vehicle swayed from side to side down the tracks. One of the candidates being considered was on the car that day, as was McKinley. Rather than helping the woman, the man shifted his newspaper to avoid seeing her. McKinley walked down the aisle, took her basket, and offered his seat to the woman. This lack of compassion made the difference. McKinley decided to appoint the other man as his ambassador.

Jesus then halted the stretcher, looked at the corpse, and said, "Young man, I say to you, arise." If this were anyone else, that would have been incredibly inappropriate and even rude, right? You can't just interrupt a funeral procession and start talking to the corpse, much less ordering it to get up. But Jesus is not anyone else. He has resurrection power! He has the divine ability to make dead things alive! — And that same power can bring life to our dead things, too. It can bring life to a dead marriage, to a dead dream, or to a dead soul. Jesus has resurrection power!

There were three times when Jesus raised someone from the dead in the gospels. Interestingly, He spoke directly to the body each time. To Jairus' daughter: "Little girl, I say to you, arise" (Mark

5:41). To Lazarus: "Lazarus, come out" (John 11:43). To this woman's son: "Young man, I say to you, arise" (Luke 7:14). If Jesus had not specified the person He wanted to raise, every person who has ever died would have come forth. And though He didn't do it then, one day Jesus will do that.

> "For the Lord himself will descend from heaven with a cry of command, with the voice of an archangel, and with the sound of the trumpet of God. And the dead in Christ will rise first" (1 Thessalonians 4:16).

The "cry of command" that Jesus will issue on the last day is for the dead to come forth.

> "Do not marvel at this, for an hour is coming when all who are in the tombs will hear his voice and come out, those who have done good to the resurrection of life, and those who have done evil to the resurrection of judgment" (John 5:28-29).

The boy immediately sat up and began to speak. Don't you wonder what he said? "Mom, what's going on here? Why is everybody looking at me? Why are you crying? Why am I on this stretcher? If I didn't know any better, I'd think this was a funeral procession!"

The reunion of this mom and her son was a foretaste of the ultimate reunion to come. Just as Jesus brought them back together, He will one day bring all those who trust in Him back together. That is why Paul could tell the Thessalonians not to grieve as the world does.

> "But we do not want you to be uninformed, brothers, about those who are asleep, that you may not grieve as others do who have no hope" (1 Thessalonians 4:13).

Christians sorrow at the loss of a loved one, but not as others do "who have no hope." Ours is one of separation, not desperation. We know the parting is temporary, and that we will one day be reunited in heaven forever. And just as Jesus wiped away this woman's tears, He will wipe away all our tears.

> "He will wipe away every tear from their eyes, and death shall be no more, neither shall there be mourning, nor crying, nor pain anymore, for the former things have passed away" (Revelation 21:4).

Do you know the difference between the resurrection of this boy and the resurrection of Jesus? I can think of three. (1) The boy eventually died again, but Jesus was raised to never die again. (2) The boy was raised by someone else's power, but Jesus was raised by His own power. (3) The boy's resurrection gave new life to him and his mother, but Jesus' resurrection can give new life to all who trust in Him. While we celebrate the resurrection of the boy from Nain, we rejoice even more in the resurrection of the One who raised the boy from Nain!

Closing

Jesus did not have to intervene. He could have just offered words of condolence or stood silently as the stretcher passed by. However, I believe Jesus was so full of compassion that He couldn't do anything other than help. Her tears flooded His spirit, and they prompted Him to halt the procession. That's grace.

A cemetery appointment was canceled. A lost son was returned to his mother. A widow's future was given stability. A broken heart was put back together. What death had stolen was reclaimed. Grace.

On that day, there were multiple collisions. (1) Two crowds collided. (2) Two only sons collided. (3) Two enemies collided — Jesus and death, which Paul calls "the last enemy" in 1 Corinthians 15:26. For the mourning mother, that site took on new significance. The gate of Nain became the gate of grace.

Grace at a Dinner

A preacher was drinking coffee in a Honolulu café one night when a group of prostitutes walked in and sat nearby. He overheard one of them, a girl named Agnes, say that her birthday was the next day and that she had never had a birthday party before. Therefore, the preacher went over and asked the café owner about the girls. He found out that they came in every night at the same time. He then asked if it would be okay to throw Agnes a surprise party the following evening. The owner agreed.

The other girls were told what the preacher planned to do and were asked to spread the word. By the next night, the café was packed with prostitutes. When Agnes walked in and saw all the streamers, balloons, and her very own birthday cake, she was overwhelmed. Tears poured down her face as the crowd sang "Happy Birthday."

A preacher throws a party for a prostitute. A man of the light celebrates with a woman of the night. Who could have imagined such a thing? Some preachers would not even make eye-contact with a woman like that, much less mingle with them. Yet this man went out of his way to show love and compassion. He sacrificed his time, his money, and possibly his reputation for someone who had done absolutely nothing to deserve it. That's grace.

After the Watergate scandal, disgraced former-President Richard Nixon returned to Washington for Hubert Humphrey's funeral. The other dignitaries made it obvious that he was not welcome there. They all shunned him. One man said that Nixon "looked like he was four feet tall, all shrunk up in himself, and gray as a ghost." However, when sitting-President Jimmy Carter entered the room and saw Nixon standing alone, he immediately walked over to him, held out his hand with a smile, and said, "Welcome home, Mr. President! Welcome home!" Carter was from a different political party and knew how everyone in the room felt about Nixon. Yet he went out of his way to show compassion. That's grace.

And there's another interesting facet to that story. Hubert Humphrey and Richard Nixon were bitter political rivals. They had squared off in the 1968 presidential election, which was one of the closest and most hard-fought elections in history. Yet shortly before Humphrey passed away, he arranged for Nixon to attend his funeral and insisted that he receive the full honor due a former President. More grace.

Jesus spent His whole life showing grace to the disgraced. From touching a leper to speaking to a Samaritan woman to eating with tax collectors, He was the personification of "loving the unloved" and extending favor to those who least deserve it. One of my favorite examples of this is found in Luke 7:36-48.

"One of the Pharisees asked him to eat with him, and he went into the Pharisee's house and reclined at table. And behold, a woman of the city, who was a sinner, when she learned that he was reclining at table in the Pharisee's house, brought an alabaster flask of ointment, and standing behind him at his feet, weeping, she began to wet his feet with her tears and wiped them with the hair of her head and kissed his feet and anointed them with the ointment. Now when the Pharisee who had invited him saw this, he said to himself, 'If this man were a prophet, he would have known who and what sort of woman this is who is touching him, for she is a sinner.' And Jesus answering said to him, 'Simon, I have something to say to you.' And he answered, 'Say it, Teacher.' 'A certain moneylender had two debtors. One owed five hundred denarii, and the other fifty. When they could not pay, he cancelled the debt of both. Now which of them will love him more?' Simon answered, 'The one, I suppose, for whom he cancelled the larger debt.' And he said to him, 'You have judged rightly.' Then turning toward the woman he said to Simon, 'Do you see this woman? I entered your house; you gave me no water for my feet, but she has wet my feet with her tears and wiped them with her hair. You gave me no kiss, but from the time I came in she has not ceased to kiss my feet. You did not anoint my head with oil, but she has anointed my feet with ointment. Therefore I tell you, her sins, which are many, are forgiven — for she loved much. But he who is forgiven little, loves little.' And he said to her, 'Your sins are forgiven.'"

The "Pharisees" were one of three major sects that existed among the Jews in the first century, along with the Sadducees and Essenes. They were known for their strict observance of oral tradition in addition to the Old Law. The Jewish historian Josephus put it like this:

"The Pharisees have delivered to the people a great many observances by succession from their fathers, which are not written in the law of Moses" (*Antiquities*, 13:10).

To the Pharisees, the Old Law was not enough. They felt that their tradition was also necessary and equally-binding. For instance, the Old Law said that Jews were not to work on the Sabbath. Their tradition then defined what classified as "work." — You could not walk more than seven-tenths of a mile, take the saddle off your donkey, or take medicine for a sore throat. If a hen laid an egg on the Sabbath, you couldn't eat it because she had worked that day. — This was not what the Old Law said, it was what their tradition stipulated; and they demanded that people strictly adhere to it.

Pharisaic tradition was so strenuous that it became "defiling" to even touch items that could be used for work on the Sabbath, like a hammer or saw. It wasn't that you were doing work, but you were touching something that could be used for doing work and therefore it was wrong. As you might expect, the Pharisees were often at odds with Jesus because He was free of their tradition and would not abide by their code. Though many in Jewish society submitted to their legalism, Jesus never did.

There were some instances, however, when certain Pharisees reached out to Jesus. Their motives may not always have been sincere, but they at least pretended to be kind. This is one of those times. A Pharisee named Simon invited the Lord over for dinner.

In that day, when someone was entertaining a prominent guest, like a rabbi, they would leave the door open and allow others to come inside and listen to the conversation. These people were not active participants, but silent observers. They would just linger along the wall in the shadows trying to be as inconspicuous as possible.

At some point during the dinner, a woman slipped into the room holding an expensive bottle of perfume. We are not told her name, but she did have a reputation of being very immoral, possibly a prostitute (TLB). Rather than being discreet like the other onlookers, the woman came over to the table and began weeping at the Lord's feet. She even let down her hair to wipe up the tears, which was considered inappropriate for women to do. This behavior embarrassed the Pharisee and made him quite angry. He snarled inwardly, "If this man were a prophet, he would have known who and what sort of woman this is touching him, for she is a sinner."

There is a scene in the movie "Home Alone" where Kevin lunges at his brother Buzz who was teasing him, causing several drinks to spill in the crowded kitchen. Milk covers the passports and a Pepsi pours onto the table and into everyone's lap. His uncle then yells, "Look what you did, you little jerk," and they all stare at Kevin in utter disgust. That's how the mood must have been at Simon's house when the conversation was interrupted by this woman. The shock quickly gave way to seething indignation. Everyone probably just stared at her in utter disgust!

Jesus was aware of what Simon and everyone else in the room was thinking. He knew that they were all appalled at this woman and were expecting Him to rebuke her. After all, she was a notorious sinner who had violated social decorum. (She slipped in uninvited, interrupted the dinner, and let her hair down in public). There was a lot of pressure on Jesus to condemn this woman and send her away in shame. Yet He chose to be merciful to her and rebuke the host. He pointed out to Simon that he had omitted even the basic forms of hospitality, like providing water for his guest's feet, while this woman had wet His feet with her tears and wiped them with her hair. Rather than condemning the woman, Jesus commended her. That's grace.

On a wintery night in 1935, Mayor Fiorello LaGuardia of New York showed up for night court in the poorest ward of the city. He dismissed the judge and took over the bench. An old woman was brought before him charged with stealing a loaf of bread. She defended herself by saying, "My daughter's husband has deserted her.

She is sick and her children are starving." The shopkeeper refused to drop the charges and demanded justice.

LaGuardia fined the woman ten dollars for her offense. As he was pronouncing the sentence, however, he reached into his pocket and took out a ten-dollar bill to pay the fine. He then said, "Here's the ten dollars you owe. Now I am going to fine everyone in this courtroom fifty cents for living in a town where a person must steal bread so that her grandchildren can eat. Mr. Bailiff, collect the fines and give them to the defendant."

LaGuardia did not excuse the woman's crime, but he did have mercy on her and drew attention to the fact that she was not the only culprit in the room. His response was a lot like that of Jesus in this account. He did not ignore the woman's sins but was merciful, while pointing out the shameful behavior taking place around her.

What upset Jesus most in this story was the Pharisee's self-righteousness. He had a spiritual smugness that blinded him to his own shortcomings. He could not see any fault in himself, though he was very good at finding fault in others. This seems to have been a common characteristic of many Pharisees (Luke 18:9-14). On the other hand, the woman demonstrated a humble and contrite spirit. She was a broken vessel and made no attempt to hide that fact.

> "The sacrifice you desire is a broken spirit. You will not reject a broken and repentant heart, O God" (Psalm 51:17, NLT).

A man was speaking to about 200 people during a seminar. He held up a $20 bill and asked, "Who wants this?" Everyone's hand immediately went up in the air. He then crumpled up the $20 bill and asked, "Who wants this now?" The hands remained in the air. He proceeded to drop the $20 bill on the ground and grind it with his shoe as he asked, "How about now?" Still the room was full of raised hands. That is because the crumpled and dirty $20 bill had not lost its value. It was still worth something.

There are times in life when poor decisions leave us crumpled and dirty. We are no longer crisp or finely-creased like before. However, that does not mean we have lost our worth to God. He still sees value in us even when we have made mistakes and been tattered by our transgressions. The way Jesus handled this immoral woman is certainly proof of that!

Closing

It has been said, "Grace does not permit us to do wrong, it allows us to be right." I have no doubt that the Lord's merciful response to this immoral woman allowed her to walk out of that room with a new purpose in life. The burden of sin and shame and sorrow had finally been lifted. His bold act of grace turned "impossible" into "I'm possible!"

Grace on a Roadside

Human eyes are incredible. They are composed of millions of working parts and are the second most complex organs we have. The muscles in our eyes are the most active part of the body and are 100 times stronger than they need to be to perform their function. Our eyes can see 500 shades of grey and, in the right conditions and lighting, can see a candle burning 14 miles away. Our eyes are capable of processing 36,000 pieces of information in a single hour and will see over 24 million different images in an average lifespan. One reason God gave us two eyeballs is for depth perception. The comparative images allow us to determine the distance of an object. Sadly, however, there are about 39 million blind people in the world, and roughly six times that many have some kind of visual impairment.

One of my best friends, Chris Peltz, is blind. He began losing his vision as a teenager and within a few years could no longer see at all. Chris has never seen his wife, his children, or me. However, one of the things I admire most about my friend is that he has never let his disability disable him. He has never used blindness as an excuse in my presence. He still cooks, cleans, hunts (yes, you read that correctly), and preaches the gospel. He even runs a non-profit organization to help first-responders and military personnel who have lost their sight.

My friend, and the millions of other people who struggle with vision impairment, are in good company. The apostle Paul also had eye trouble. There are several indications of this in Scripture:

- ☐ Paul could not see that it was the high priest before him (Acts 23:5).
- ☐ Paul had to rely on others to write his epistles (Romans 16:22).
- ☐ Paul suffered from a "thorn in the flesh" (2 Corinthians 12:7).
- ☐ Paul said the Galatians would have gouged out their eyes and given them to him (Galatians 4:15).
- ☐ When Paul did write parts of his epistles, he used very large letters (Galatians 6:11).

The evidence seems to prove that Paul had difficulty seeing. Yet he still did tremendous work for the Lord, saving souls, establishing congregations, and writing almost half of the New Testament. Like my friend Chris, he did not let his disability disable him!

The Lord encountered many blind men during His earthly ministry. On one occasion, as Jesus was making His way toward Jerusalem for the Passover, He came across a blind man just outside of Jericho. It was a remarkable meeting that transformed the man's life forever. The account is recorded in all three synoptic gospels. We will look at Mark's account.

"And they came to Jericho. And as he was leaving Jericho with his disciples and a great crowd, Bartimaeus, a blind beggar, the son of Timaeus, was sitting by the roadside. And when he heard that it was Jesus of Nazareth, he began to cry out and say, 'Jesus, Son of David, have mercy on me!' And many rebuked him, telling him to be silent. But he cried out all the more, 'Son of David, have mercy on me!' And Jesus stopped and said, 'Call him.' And they called the blind man, saying to him, 'Take heart. Get up; he is calling you.' And throwing off his cloak, he sprang up and came to Jesus. And Jesus said to him, 'What do you want me to do for you?' And the blind man said to him, 'Rabbi, let me recover my sight.' And Jesus said to him, 'Go your way; your faith has made you well.' And immediately he recovered his sight and followed him on the way" (Mark 10:46-52).

Jill and I were in different parts of a store when she walked up to me and said, "I want to show you something I think you'll like over here. Close your eyes." I reluctantly grabbed her shoulder, shut my eyes, and we began to move. As we were walking, I thought to myself, "Wow! This is a lot harder — and scarier — than I imagined." I put my free hand out as a buffer and worried that I might hit a pole or knock something over. It was a reminder of the challenges blind people face daily.

As hard as it is being blind today, it was even more difficult in the first century. First, the roads and villages were not very "handicap accessible." Their streets were unpaved with holes and rocks, and there were no sidewalks, audible crossing signals, or trained guide dogs to assist the visually impaired. Second, most blind people had no means of support and were reduced to begging on the streets. Third, there was a social and religious stigma attached to blindness. It was thought that disabilities were the consequence of some sin. In fact, even the disciples had that misconception.

> "As he passed by, he saw a man blind from birth. And his disciples asked him, 'Rabbi, who sinned, this man or his parents, that he was born blind?' Jesus answered, 'It was not that this man sinned, or his parents, but that the works of God might be displayed in him'" (John 9:1-3).

In that society, blindness was often viewed as recompense for sin. They assumed the person was being punished. "He's just getting what he deserves" was the mindset of many. This made matters even worse for those with this disability. We should note, however, that the Old Law instructed God's people to be compassionate to the blind.

> "You shall not curse the deaf or put a stumbling block before the blind, but you shall fear your God: I am the Lord" (Leviticus 19:14).

Though Matthew says that there was a second blind man present, Mark focuses on the one who was more visible and vocal — Bartimaeus. He didn't have a rich uncle, trust fund, or government program to support him, so he was forced to do what most blind people did to survive. He sat on the roadside asking for money. He was a blind beggar!

With Passover drawing near, the road from Jericho to Jerusalem would have been more crowded than usual. It is conservatively-estimated that about 200,000 Jews made the trip each year. (Some estimates are much higher than that). And most of the travelers were probably in a good mood, feeling festive and generous. This was an ideal place for a beggar to position himself.

The commotion of Jesus approaching with a large crowd of people did not go unnoticed by Bartimaeus. He perked up to hear what was going on and asked those around him who was passing by. When he found out it was Jesus, he began crying out, "Jesus, Son of David, have mercy on me!" This was his chance and he was not going to squander it.

When I was a teenager, my dad put a picture on my bedroom wall of a boy with a basketball looking up at the goal. The caption read, "You miss 100% of the shots you don't take." Bartimaeus wasn't going to miss his opportunity to score. He seized the moment by calling out to Jesus. He was not asking for money, but for mercy. He didn't want a handout, but a hand up. Bartimaeus desired to be healed and clearly believed in the Lord's ability to do it.

We are not given details about Bartimaeus' appearance, but it is easy to imagine how he probably looked. He was covered in dust and wearing raggedy clothes. His hair was tangled, his skin was blotchy, his teeth were crooked, his toenails were cracked, and he reeked of body odor. To most people, he was nothing more than a disgusting stain on society. That may be why they told him to "shut up" (LB) when he called out to the Lord.

Has that ever happened to you? Have you ever faced opposition for letting your faith in Jesus be known? Perhaps it came from an un-believing spouse, an annoyed co-worker, or a guilt-stricken sinner. They didn't like your devotion to the Lord and tried to get you to "tone it down." If so, the example of Bartimaeus should be of great encouragement. He ignored the noise around him by making some noise of his own. When they yelled, he just yelled louder! And Jesus rewarded him for his resolve.

We do not know if Jesus had already noticed Bartimaeus or not. Maybe He was just waiting for the blind beggar to make the first move. What we do know is that amid all the clamoring, Jesus heard his cry and was receptive to it. He stopped in His tracks and asked the man to come near. *The Message* paraphrase says they told Bar-timaeus, "It's your lucky day! Get up! He's calling for you to come!"

Bartimaeus wasted no time. He threw off his cloak and hurried over to Jesus. The symbolism of throwing off the cloak is powerful. That cloak was probably his blanket at night and served as his protection from the sun during the day. And though he surely threw it off for a practical reason (he didn't want to trip over it), it figuratively represents his past life. He was leaving that behind to answer the call of the Lord. He now had a new focus and new priority. His hopeless despair was giving way to healing and deliverance. It is reminiscent of the Samaritan woman "leaving her water jar" in John 4:28. In both cases, they now had a greater purpose in life!

Jesus asked Bartimaeus, "What do you want me to do for you?" The blind man didn't have to think twice about how to answer that question. He immediately expressed his desire to see. He said, "Rabbi, let me recover my sight." And he was instantly healed. Matthew adds that Jesus "in pity" touched both men's eyes (v. 34). Bartimaeus went from wallowing to following. He became a disciple at that very moment.

Once again, we see the transformational power of grace. The chains of darkness that had bound Bartimaeus for so long were broken in pieces by the overwhelming light of Jesus. He once was blind, but now could see!

Closing

On November 30, 1991, a severe dust storm triggered a massive pileup along Interstate 5 in California. At least 14 people died and dozens more were injured as visibility was reduced to zero. The dust storm left a three-mile trail of twisted and burning vehicles in its wake. Sadly, the world is full of people who have been blinded by a spiritual dust storm and have no idea that they are heading straight for destruction. Satan has "covered their minds so they cannot see" (2 Corinthians 4:4, WE). Yet Jesus offers to restore their sight and save them from the coming catastrophe, if they will but seek Him in humble obedience. Just as it is impossible to sneeze with your eyes open, it is impossible to be saved without the Lord. Bartimaeus received His grace, will you?

Grace at a Tree

"I don't care how much that job pays, it's not worth it." Have you ever had a thought like that before? A time when you said to yourself, "Regardless of how much a person might make in that particular profession, the amount of stress or danger or time or creepiness or embarrassment involved totally outweighs the income? It's just not worth it." Some of the jobs that I would put on that list are embalmer, astronaut, stunt man, stenographer, brain surgeon, state executioner, and the guy who changes that light bulb at the top of those tall towers. — I don't care how much that job pays, I don't want it!

This one, however, might top the cake. I learned of this job from an article entitled, "My job stinks:' The diver who has to swim through sewers to unblock the drains of Mexico City." It was published online back in 2013. Here is an excerpt:

> "Julio Cu Camara's day job is dirty work. The 52-year-old spends his working days submerged in the murky liquid of Mexico City's sewers, clearing blockages and carrying out repairs by hand.

For 30 years, Cu Camara has made an average of four dives a month, staying below the surface for about 30 minutes to six hours at a time.

He wears an airtight suit and helmet that weigh about 90lb in total to protect him from the human, chemical and animal waste and its overpowering stench.

Cu Camara has encountered dead human bodies, horses and pigs as well as weapons and car parts while exploring a drainage system measuring about 7,456 miles long."

— Ding, ding, ding. We have a winner, right?

If we lived back in the first century, a job that would have probably made my list was "tax collector." It came with a lot of authority and paid well, but the stigma attached to it made the job undesirable. Tax collectors were viewed as traitors, for selling out their country to work for the hated Roman Empire; and they were considered to be crooks, because they often took more money than the law actually required to fatten their own pockets. That's why when some of the tax collectors came to John the Baptist in Luke 3 and asked what they should do, he responded, "Collect no more taxes than you are authorized to do." They were known for extorting people!

Tax collectors were barred from the synagogue and could not testify in court. They ranked with unclean animals and prostitutes in the mind of most Jews, and they were referred to as "beasts in human shape." Even their money was considered tainted and thought to defile anyone who accepted it.

Jesus encountered many tax collectors during His earthly ministry, but one such encounter was especially significant. It occurred about a week before His crucifixion and is found only in the Gospel of Luke.

> "He entered Jericho and was passing through. And behold, there was a man named Zacchaeus. He was a chief tax collector and was rich. And he was seeking to see who Jesus was, but on account of the crowd he could not, because he was small in stature. So he ran on ahead and climbed up into a sycamore tree to see him, for he was about to pass that way. And when Jesus came to the place, he looked up and said to him, 'Zacchaeus, hurry and come down, for I must stay at your house today.' So he hurried and came down and received him joyfully. And when they saw it, they all grumbled, 'He has gone in to be the guest of a man who is a sinner.' And Zacchaeus stood and said to the Lord, 'Behold, Lord, the half of my goods I give to the poor. And if I have defrauded anyone of anything, I restore it fourfold.' And Jesus said to him, 'Today salvation has come to

this house, since he also is a son of Abraham. For the Son of Man came to seek and to save the lost'" (Luke 19:1-10).

"Jericho" was located about 15 miles northeast of Jerusalem and not far from the Jordan River. It was a prosperous town in the first century and home to a supervisor of tax collectors named Zacchaeus. He was a wealthy man.

The name "Zacchaeus" means "pure" or "righteous," but his profession and reputation suggest that he was not living up to his name. Verse 7 says that he was known as a "sinner." Zacchaeus was no doubt an extortionist who abused his power for personal gain, just like other tax collectors.

In addition to taking more than required, tax collectors loaned money at excessively high rates of interest to those who were unable to pay their taxes. They were basically first century loan sharks! They would also hire thugs to physically intimidate people into paying, and to beat up those who refused.

Though tax collecting may have been lucrative, it was a very isolating occupation. Zacchaeus would have been shunned by the people of his town. They would have given him the silent treatment in the market and not let their kids play with his at the park. Mrs. Zacchaeus would not have been invited out to lunch by the other moms, either. Their social circle probably only consisted of other tax collectors. William Barclay wrote,

"Zacchaeus was wealthy but not happy. Inevitably he was lonely, for he had chosen a way that made him an outcast" (*Luke*, p. 234).

Perhaps that was an underlying reason why Zacchaeus came to see Jesus. Could it have been more than mere curiosity or boredom that prompted him to "sneak a peek?" I can't help but think that Zacchaeus was a lonely, unfulfilled soul who was searching for something.

A lot of people have the mistaken idea that their lives would be full and happy if only they had more money. They think wealth would solve all their problems and fill that nagging void in their soul. But such is not the case. Some of the emptiest people I have ever met had full bank accounts.

Robin Williams was worth an estimated $50 million dollars when he committed suicide in 2014. Rock stars, professional athletes, and successful businessmen have all suffered from severe depression and anxiety, and in some cases killed themselves, despite having enormous fame and fortune. As Solomon, who was extremely well-to-do himself, wrote,

> "He who loves money will not be satisfied with money, nor he who loves wealth with his income; this also is vanity" (Ecclesiastes 5:10).

Though we are not told much about Zacchaeus, we do know that he was a short man; small in stature. In fact, that is probably the thing he is most known for today due to the popular kid's song, "Zacchaeus Was A Wee Little Man." He was the tiny tax collector!

As Jesus drew near, Zacchaeus did two things that were very uncommon for men of his status to do: (1) he ran down the street, and (2) he climbed up in a tree. Luke tells us that it was a "sycamore tree," which had a short trunk with low branches. Zacchaeus was determined to see Jesus.

The first line of verse 3 says, "And he was seeking to see who Jesus was, but on account of the crowd he could not." Notice that the people made it hard for Zacchaeus to get a good look at Jesus. Could we be guilty of that in the church today? Do we sometimes make it hard for people to see Jesus? — Perhaps it's hypocrisy in our own lives, or a lack of enthusiasm for the gospel, or a self-righteous attitude that turns people off. Maybe we bind our opinions on others and then make condescending remarks when they don't fall in line. — We need to be careful that our actions and attitudes don't turn people off and "get in the way" of them seeing Jesus. We want to clear their view, not cloud it!

To his credit, Zacchaeus got above the crowd. He didn't let them hold him back or keep him away. He climbed up in the sycamore tree and positioned himself to get a good look at the Lord. This allowed him to be seen as well.

When Jesus arrived at the tree, He did three things that must have shocked Zacchaeus and everyone in the crowd: (1) he stopped, (2) he looked up, and (3) he called the man by name. Had they ever met? Probably not. Yet Jesus addressed him not as "gentleman" or "sir" or "sinner," but as "Zacchaeus." Then Jesus did something even more shocking; He invited Himself over for dinner!

What if Jesus showed up at your house unannounced? Would you be tickled or terrified by that? Would you be able to invite Him right inside, or would He have to wait on the front porch while you turned off the questionable movie you were watching or hid the SI swimsuit edition lying on the counter? Would your kids look stunned when you bowed to pray before eating? Would you struggle to carry on a conversation about spiritual things? Would you have to discreetly tell your teenage daughter to "go put on more clothes" when she walked in with friends? — What if Jesus showed up at your house? Zacchaeus had no warning that Jesus was coming over, but he was ready to receive Him when He did.

Zacchaeus hurried out of the tree to play host. It didn't matter what appointments he had on the calendar for that afternoon, they could be rescheduled. He had a more pressing obligation. He was going home to entertain a very special guest! And that left the crowd reeling.

> "And when they saw it, they all grumbled, 'He has
> gone in to be the guest of a man who is a sinner'"
> (v. 7).

No self-respecting Jew would dare pollute himself by going into the house of a tax collector. It was taboo. You just didn't do that. It would have garnered the same reaction as walking into a known crack house today. And the crowd certainly let their disapproval be known. *The Message* paraphrase puts it like this:

> "Everyone who saw the incident was indignant and grumped, 'What business does he have getting cozy with this crook?'"

The crowd's reaction was similar to that of the older brother in the Parable of the Prodigal Son. He too resented that grace was being extended to someone so "morally inferior" to himself.

Zacchaeus became a guest in his own house, for Jesus was now his Master. He was ready to serve and obey the Lord. He even offered to make restitution to those he defrauded, which is what genuine repentance requires. "I'll restore it fourfold," he said.

A group of women were talking about how Jesus had changed their lives, but one woman just sat there silently. She was asked to participate but refused to do so. When they asked her why, she answered, "Four of these women who have testified owe me money, and my family is half-starved because we can't afford food." — You see, a testimony is worthless until it is backed up by action. Jesus does not want chatter, He wants change. Zacchaeus knew that!

Someone can say they love Jesus all day long, but do their actions bear that out? Do they give generously? Attend regularly? Pray consistently? Are they growing in their faith and love or have they become spiritually stagnant? It's one thing to "talk the talk," but it is something altogether different to "walk the walk."

Max Lucado, in his book on grace, wrote, "Have you been changed by grace? Shaped by grace? Emboldened by grace? Softened by grace? Snatched by the nape of your neck and shaken to your senses by grace? Grace is the voice that calls us to change and then gives us the power to pull it off" (p. 9). — Zacchaeus was now living proof of that. Though he may not have had all the details worked out yet, his direction was now set. When Jesus entered the front door, corruption and greed ran out the back. Grace prevailed!

Interestingly, the only other tax collector named in the New Testament is Levi, who is better known to us as the apostle Matthew. And both men were converted to Christ! This demonstrates that no one is beyond the grasp of the gospel; that no one is too bad or too far gone to be saved. If it could reach despised tax collectors, then it can reach anybody!

Closing

Zacchaeus appeared to be an unlikely prospect for the gospel. He was rich, reviled, and ruthless. Before climbing that tree, he had climbed the ladder of success on the backs of his own people. He put lucre above loyalty by working for the Roman Empire and seemed to be concerned only with himself. Yet there was something missing in his life; a void that nothing could fill but Jesus. And once again, we see that God's grace was greater than his disgrace!

Grace on a Cross

Have you ever heard of Judas the Galilean? He is mentioned in the book of Acts (5:37) and by the historian Josephus. Judas was a Jewish man who strongly opposed Roman taxation and urged his people to rise up against their oppressors. He led a violent revolt that ultimately failed, though it did result in the establishment of a new sect called the "Zealots."

Judas the Galilean was captured and sentenced to death. He was stripped of his clothes, tied to a pole, and repeatedly struck with a whip that had sharp objects attached to its thongs. This lashing tore open his skin and left his body limp and bloody. Then he was forced to his feet and taken to an area where executions were performed. There he was nailed to a cross and left to die.

Jesus would have heard about Judas the Galilean while growing up. He would have known what kind of punishment Judas suffered at the hands of the Roman Empire and, at some point, realized that He would experience a similar death one day — not for calling men to revolt, but for calling them to repent.

Jesus made it abundantly clear during His earthly ministry that He knew what was coming. On several occasions, He warned the apostles that He would be put to death.

> "From that time Jesus began to show his disciples that he must go to Jerusalem and suffer many things from the elders and chief priests and scribes, and be killed, and on the third day be raised" (Matthew 16:21).

> "As they were gathering in Galilee, Jesus said to them, 'The Son of Man is about to be delivered into the hands of men, and they will kill him, and he will be raised on the third day'" (Matthew 17:22-23).

> "And as Jesus was going up to Jerusalem, he took the twelve disciples aside, and on the way he said to them, 'See, we are going up to Jerusalem. And the Son of Man will be delivered over to the chief priests and scribes, and they will condemn him to death, and deliver him over to the Gentiles to be mocked and flogged and crucified, and he will be raised on the third day'" (Matthew 20:17-19).

A French philosopher once said, "My life has been filled with terrible misfortune; most of which never happened." I think many of us can relate with that. Studies show that 85% of the things we worry about do not come to pass. — "What if I have a brain freeze and fail the entrance exam?" "What if my son breaks his leg playing football?" "What if my company decides to relocate to another city?"

"What if the new neighbors like to party and keep us up at night?"
"What if the thing I am worrying about isn't part of the 85%?"

Whereas we tend to worry about things that will not come to pass, Jesus didn't worry about things that would come to pass. Have you ever thought about that? He was still happy and functional, despite knowing that a thorny crown, two cross beams, and three iron nails were in His future. He just trusted in God and lived carefree. We are told to do the same.

> "Live carefree before God; he is most careful with you" (1 Peter 5:7, MSG).

When that day finally arrived, Jesus went through the same thing as Judas the Galilean. He was seized, scourged, and spiked. Let's look at Luke's account:

> "And when they came to the place that is called The Skull, there they crucified him, and the criminals, one on his right and one on his left" (Luke 23:33).

None of the four gospel writers go into detail about crucifixion. That is probably because their original audience would have already been familiar with it. At that time, crucifixions were common and carried out in public for all to see. However, I think it is important for us to be reminded of what we're talking about.

The *International Standard Encyclopedia* has one of the best descriptions of crucifixion I have read. It says,

> "Among the Romans crucifixion was preceded by scourging, undoubtedly to hasten impending death. The victim then bore his own cross, or at least the upright beam, to the place of execution... The suffering of death by crucifixion was intense, esp. in hot climates. Severe local inflammation, coupled with an insignificant bleeding of the jagged wounds, produced traumatic fever, which was aggravated by the exposure to the heat of the sun, the strained position of the body and insufferable thirst. The wounds swelled about the rough nails and the torn and lacerated tendons and nerves caused excruciating agony. The arteries of the head and stomach were surcharged with blood and a terrific throbbing headache ensued. The mind was confused and filled with anxiety and dread foreboding. The victim of crucifixion literally died a thousand deaths. Tetanus not rarely supervened and the rigors of the attending convulsions would tear at the wounds and add to the burden of pain, till at last the bodily forces were exhausted and the victim sank to unconsciousness and death" (ISBE, p. 761).

It is my understanding that the nails were 6-7 inches long. The horizontal cross beam that Jesus carried was about 6 feet long and weighed around 70 pounds. It was an unfinished piece of lumber, which means its splintery surface would have rubbed against His open wounds. The vertical cross beam was about 8 feet long. Jesus was on the cross for 6 hours.

Luke tells us that Jesus was not the only person crucified that day. There were two other condemned prisoners being executed. Matthew and Mark tell us they were "robbers." One was positioned on the right side of Jesus, and the other on His left. And at first, they both hurled insults at the Lord.

> "And the robbers who were crucified with him also reviled him in the same way" (Matthew 27:44).

The two robbers deserved to be there. They were guilty of crimes that merited death. However, Jesus was the innocent Son of God, dying on a cross originally intended for someone else. It had been prepared for another Jesus.

Just hours earlier, Jesus Barabbas was sitting in a Jerusalem jail cell trying to prepare himself for death. He had said his goodbyes and eaten his final meal. He knew there was no chance of a commuted sentence for a guy with a rap sheet like his — robbery, murder, insurrection. Matthew calls him a "notorious prisoner." Yet a man named Jesus of Nazareth seemed to emerge with the morning light to take his place. A custom called the "Paschal Pardon" allowed the people to free the worst Pilate could offer and condemn the best God could offer. One Jesus for the other. Barabbas was the first person to benefit from the Lord's sacrifice.

While on the cross, Jesus remained mostly silent as the religious leaders, the Roman soldiers, and the two robbers railed at Him. He maintained self-control, despite being relentlessly taunted and teased. He was also extremely uncomfortable. Though every part of His body was aching, He kept His composure. Peter put it like this:

> "When he was reviled, he did not revile in return; when he suffered, he did not threaten, but continued entrusting himself to him who judges justly" (1 Peter 2:23).

At some point, one of the robbers had a change of heart. We don't know what sparked it — whether it was the sobering reality of death approaching or the honorable example of Jesus — but his attitude went from repulsion to repentance. His haughtiness gave way to humility.

> "One of the criminals who were hanged railed at him, saying, 'Are you not the Christ? Save yourself and us!' But the other rebuked him, saying, 'Do you not fear God, since you are under the same sentence of condemnation? And we indeed justly, for we are receiving the due reward of our deeds; but this man has done nothing wrong.' And he said, 'Jesus, remember me when you come into your kingdom.' And he said to him, 'Truly, I say to you, today you

will be with me in paradise'" (Luke 23:39-43).

"Paradise" is sometimes used of heaven (Revelation 2:7), but here it refers to a place of comfort in the hadean realm. "Hades" is the abode of the dead; it is where disembodied spirits remain until the Second Coming of Christ. Hades is described for us in Luke 16:19-31. Jesus promised the penitent robber that they would soon be together in paradise!

Perhaps you are wondering how we know that Jesus and the robber went to Hades and not to heaven that day. We know that because of what Peter said on the day of Pentecost. He explained,

> "For David says concerning him… For you will not abandon my soul to Hades, or let your Holy One see corruption… He foresaw and spoke about the resurrection of Christ, that he was not abandoned to Hades, nor did his flesh see corruption" (Acts 2: 25, 27, 31).

Here we have some divine commentary. One passage helps to interpret the other. Peter said that Jesus' soul went to Hades when He died, though it did not stay there long enough for His body to decay. Hence, the promise of paradise in Luke 23 is not referring to heaven, but Hades.

The Lord's promise to the penitent robber implies two things: (1) there is consciousness after death, and (2) there is recognition after death. This refutes the doctrine of soul-sleeping or annihilation.

Jesus did not mention the robber's past transgressions or even his earlier insults on the cross. There were no stern rebukes, rehashing of past mistakes, or demands for a public apology. Like the father of the Prodigal, He just tenderly welcomed his repentance. That's grace.

This man had been an embarrassment to his family, a stain on society, and an inmate on death row. He was more than a petty thief; he was a menacing bandit. He had probably resorted to violence in the commission of his crimes and left a wake of terror in his path. Yet he was not too bad to be saved. That's grace.

When Jesus was on earth, He would sometimes verbally pronounce that a person's sins had been forgiven. He did that with the crippled man in Mark 2 and with the notorious sinner in Luke 7, and the same is certainly implied with the robber in Luke 23. Now that the Great Commission is in effect, forgiveness is obtained by believing and being baptized (Mark 16:16). However, the fact that this salvation is by grace has not changed. None of us deserve it, yet it has been freely given!

It is hard to be graceful when you're uncomfortable. — Maybe you're stuck in traffic with no air conditioning or crammed into a crowded waiting room or forced to carry on a conversation with a splitting headache. — At times like that, it doesn't take much to lose your patience and become greatly annoyed. That is what makes this particular demonstration of grace all the more impressive. Jesus had been sentenced to death for crimes He didn't commit, He was hanging on a cross in the hot sun (at least for three of those hours), His legs were cramped, His lips were cracked, He was struggling to breathe, He was being bothered by insects, and He had sweat dripping into His eyes. Moreover, the very people He had come to save were hurling insults at Him. You talk about uncomfortable! And yet He was still extending grace to others.

Closing

There were three crosses on Golgotha that day. One was a cross of rebellion. One was a cross of repentance. And standing between them was a cross of redemption. What side of the Lord's cross are you on? Rebellion or Repentance — the choice is yours!

Closing

In 1830, a man named George Wilson was sentenced to death by hanging for mail theft. President Andrew Jackson gave Wilson a pardon, but he refused to accept it. This puzzled the authorities who did not know whether Wilson should be freed or hanged. Finally, the Supreme Court ruled that a pardon is an act of grace which must be received to be completed. Without that acceptance, it is of no effect. Therefore, George Wilson was ordered to be hanged.

All of us have sinned and fallen short of God's glory. The sentence for this crime is eternal death. Yet Jesus Christ came to earth, lived a perfect life, and was sacrificed on the cross so we could be pardoned. It is being freely offered as an act of grace. However, we must accept the pardon for it to be completed. We do that through an obedient faith.

Just as Noah was pardoned from death by flood *when* he built the ark (Genesis 6) and the Israelites were pardoned from death by snakebite *when* they looked on the bronze serpent (Numbers 21), we are pardoned from eternal death *when* we repent and are baptized (Acts 2). Have you done that?

www.ingramcontent.com/pod-product-compliance
Lightning Source LLC
Chambersburg PA
CBHW071057040426
42443CB00013B/3365